SONGS OF
Wales

51 favourite songs for voice and piano

Arranged by Margery Hargest Jones

Boosey & Hawkes Music Publishers Ltd

www.boosey.com

Introduction

The songs in this collection are taken from the original *Songs of Wales*, published by Boosey & Co. in 1873 and edited by Brinley Richards (1819-1885). It was a remarkably successful publication and became known as the national song book of Wales. In his preface Brinley Richards says that he was 'at great pains to give the tunes according to the best authorities'. Many tunes were taken 'by permission, from Miss Jane Williams' (Aberpergwm) valuable collection of national airs' of 1837. He goes on to say that Miss Williams went to a great deal of effort to add to that collection, in 1844, from 'the songs of the peasantry in the Vale of Neath, many national airs thus having been saved'.

Richards says, 'Many of the Welsh airs are very ancient and were composed before the time of Queen Elizabeth [I]: others are of more recent origin'. Among the latter included here are *There Lived a Bachelor* (1803) and *One Bright Summer Morning* (1804), both composed by John Parry (Bardd Alaw). *The Lady of Sker* was composed by Thomas Evans (died 1819), a Welsh harper from Carmarthen – 'this plaintive melody' again taken from the collection of Miss Jane Williams.

In preparing the present edition, the songs in this album have been newly arranged for voice and piano with the melody line in the accompaniment, so that the songs may be played as keyboard solos as well as with the voice. It was also considered important that the words be carefully updated, both to make them closer to the sense of the Welsh versions and to modernise the vocabulary, making them easier to sing and understand, especially for children.

The songs fall mainly into three subject categories, with some inevitable overlap. There are songs of love – usually sad and unrequited – such as *Megan's Fair Daughter* and *A Lovely Lady Softly Sighed*; songs of love of nature and the beauty of Wales, of which *The Blackbird* and *O Mountain White* are examples; and there are songs of war and battle such as *Men of Harlech* and *Forth to the Battle*.

There are also songs which reflect the long bardic tradition of Wales. *The Hall of My Chieftain* and *The Marsh of Rhuddlan* typically tell of events in Welsh history, as do the new words to *Men of Harlech*. *David of the White Rock* and *The Rising of the Lark* are said to be written by the bard and harper David Owen (1720-49). The Welsh harp has always been the chief instrument of the bards and has long been recognized as the national instrument of Wales. *Let Now the Harp* celebrates the beauty of Wales in its music.

The beauty of Wales is ever in the minds of those Welsh men and women who are exiles from their native land. *Fair Country*, *Why Do I Just Gaze?*, *Farewell My Dear Country* and *As the Night is Approaching* are all songs full of love and longing (hiraeth) for the Welsh countryside and for the Land of Song.

Background notes have been included to many of the songs to place them in context in Welsh social and musical history.

Cover design by Peter Hobbs
Layout by Sue Clarke
Music engraved by Jack Thompson
Typeset by Linden Sheffield
Chord symbols have been included above the melody line.
A transposed version is given below the stave in smaller
type where the chords are awkward for guitarists.
The chord symbols suggested have been chosen to suit the
solo melody and do not always correspond to the
harmony of the keyboard accompaniment.

Contents

All the Day

Hob y deri danno
North Wales version

English words by Walter Maynard

This is the North Wales version of an old song of the Druids. 'Hob y deri danno' literally means 'The swine (or pig) under the oaks'.

1. All the day I sigh and say, love, 'Hob y de-ri dan-no,' Jane, sweet Jane; All the night I dream or pray, love, 'Hob y de-ri dan-no;' Jane, sweet Jane. Since the time when first we met, I noth-ing but com-

© Copyright 1992 by Boosey & Hawkes Music Publishers Ltd.

plain. Though I fear you do for-get, I hope on still in vain; All day and night I long for you, Jane, sweet Jane.

2 Often as I sigh and say, love,
'Hob y deri danno,' Jane, sweet Jane!
I ask why do you delay, love,
'Hob y deri danno,' Jane, sweet Jane.
Can it be you do not care if we should meet again?
Am I then so soon forgotten, do I love in vain?
All day and night I long for you Jane, sweet Jane.

All the Day

Hob y deri dando
South Wales version

English words by Walter Maynard

1. All the day I— sigh and say, love, 'Hob y der-ri dan - do,'

All the night I— dream or pray, love, 'Hob y der-ri dan - do;'

Since the time when first we met, I— noth - ing but com - plain,

Though I fear you_ do for-get, I hope on in vain; All_ night and day
I sigh and pray for you, dear Jane.

2 Often as I sigh and say, love,
'Hob y deri dando,'
I ask why you do delay, love,
'Hob y deri dando;'
Can it be you do not care if we should meet again?
Am I then so soon forgot, do I love in vain?
All night and day I sigh and pray for you, sweet Jane.

All Through the Night

Ar hyd y nos

English words by Margery Hargest Jones

2 Cheerful stars smile down upon you,
All through the night.
Gentle breezes blow around you,
All through the night.
Morning light will bring you gladness,
Daybreak comes to end all badness,
Sleep will take away your sadness
All through the night.

As the Night Is Approaching

Yr alltud O Gymru

Words anon.

roam; When the scenes I have loved are re - lived in my mind, With my heart full of

long-ing for those left be - hind.

2 Yes, this is the hour when alone and so blue,
   The exile looks back on the days that he knew;
   Fond memories flood into heart and to mind,
   He thinks he may never find loved ones so kind.
   In vain that for him sweetest flowers will grow,
   In vain blooms for him that soft landscape we know;
   The beauty of valleys and mountains so grand
   Makes him sigh and long for his own native land.

The Ash Grove

Llwyn On

English words by Margery Hargest Jones

ash grove it makes such a beau-ti-ful ar-bour That ev-'ry-one loves ev-'ry move-ment and sound.

2 But sad it is now to remember my lover,
And how we would wander in this lovely shade.
Fond memories linger of life with another
And of the most beautiful walks that we made;
As we strolled along on a carpet of colour,
The trees all around us provided a home;
The light through the leaves of the ash grove is spreading
But gone is my loved one and I am alone.

The Bard's Love

Cariad y Bardd

Welsh words by T. Tudno Jones
English words by Margery Hargest Jones

The bard, Hoel ap Einion, fell in love with the celebrated Myfanwy Fechan, who lived at Castel Dinas Bran, in the Vale of Llangollen around 1390. He died brokenhearted because she rejected him.

*) Hy - wel the Bard__ fell e - ver so deep - ly in love,
   was in his mu - sic in - spired__ by this great_ love,

She_ was a beau - ty,__ My -**fan - wy her name; It
His_ spi - rit breathed out__ a fierce fie - ry

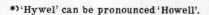

*)'Hywel' can be pronounced 'Howell'.

**) The 'f' in Myfanwy sounds as 'v'.

16

2 The crown of the Bards to him was given,
   But it was her heart that he yearned for in vain:
   Her smile was the prize for which he had striven,
   His heart was broken beneath her disdain.
   The crown on his brow was now withered and gone,
   And silent his harp and no more was his song;
   The bard had found rest and in death slumbered on.

The Bells of Aberdovey
Clychau Aberdyfi

English words by Margery Hargest Jones
Music after *Liberty Hall* by Charles Dibdin

This song was sung by a comic Welsh character in the Drury Lane opera *Liberty Hall* in 1785 and was subsequently included in many volumes of songs by the same composer. This led to it gradually being thought of as a Welsh folk song.

1. Now it's love-ly sum-mer-time,— Hear the bells ring out their rhyme,
Lis-ten to the sing-ing chime Of the bells of A-ber-do-vey. One, two, three, four,
five, six, seven, Oh lis-ten to the song of heav'n, Say the bells of A-ber-do-vey.

18

2 When at dawn we used to hear
O'er the hills their voices clear,
They would then our young hearts cheer,
Those sweet bells of Aberdovey.
One, two, three, four, five, six, seven,
O they were just a song from heav'n,
Were the bells of Aberdovey.
All their music seemed to me

Full of great mirth and measure,
As I sang so merrily
While full of joy and pleasure.
Now those days are past and gone;
Still the bells ring out ding-dong,
Singing out high heav'n's sweet song,
The bells of Aberdovey.

The Blackbird

Y Fwyalchen

English words by Margery Hargest Jones

2 A singer may sing of his gladness,
But not all of joy is his song.
There still are old mem'ries of sadness,
We hear when he is singing along.
While you have no thought of forgetting
The griefs of a long lonely past,
Your song is of joy, not regretting,
Rejoicing you sing to the last.

David of the White Rock

Dafydd y Garreg Wen

English words by Margery Hargest Jones

1. Bring me, said
2. Last night the

Da - vid, the harp I a - dore, Be - fore death
voice of an an - gel did say, 'Come home - ward

calls me, I'll play it once more, Help me to reach my be -
Da - vid for I hear you play', Harp of my youth, and your

The Dove

Y Deryn Pur

English words by Maria X. Hayes

gen - tle dove, with wing so blue, Fly quick-ly to___ my la - dy; And

take to her a mess-age true, While in her gar - den sha - dy.

Go to her and say I love her, And am try - ing to dis - co - ver

How to meet her, fond - ly greet her, But if___ my love___ should
fail to please her, May God for - give her beaut - eous face— I
know that I___ must leave her.

After Verse 2

2 With heart so gay one happy day,
   I walked with step so sprightly;
   The loveliest girl I'd ever seen
   Came tripping there so lightly.
   On her beauty so amazing
   I could only stand there gazing;
   Of the fairest, she the rarest,
   Her smile made all around her shining;
   She was an angel to my eyes,
   And for her love I'm pining.

Fair Country

Medd Merch Glyndwr

English words by Walter Maynard

find that home is there a-gain.

2 I wish such joys awaited me,
   When through the hills and vales I roam!
   I wish it were my fate to be
   The one who calls this land his own.
   The warmest welcome have I found
   From all who in that land I've met;
   I know that there kind hearts abound,
   A stranger never can forget.

Farewell My Dear Country

Yn Iach i ti Gymru

English words by Margery Hargest Jones

well to the pur-est and best of all mo-thers, O bless'd and be-lov-éd,__ dear

land of my own.

After Verse 2

2 So dear are your valleys and wild rivers flowing,
So rapid and sparkling among your green trees;
So dear are your hills in the summer sun glowing,
But dearer than all is your life-giving breeze!
Although I'll be far from the land of the wildwood,
The sky all around will remind me of home,
And of the sweet scenes of my earliest childhood;
I'll long for your peace wheresoever I roam.

Forth to the Battle

Rhwyn wrth dy Wregys

English words by Margery Hargest Jones

The first published date of this piece, also known as *Captain Morgan's March*, is 1784, when it appeared in *Musical and Poetical Relicks of the Welsh Bards* in London. It is sung to honour the winning Bards at the National Eisteddfod of Wales each August in Llangollen.

1. Forth to the bat - tle!
   March - ing to - ge - ther,

Off to fight the foe;
all a-cross the land,

Com - rades come for - ward, on we go.
Pray come and join our brave young band.

Dry your tears and hear the ar-rows fly, Mur-mur-ing their mess - age

2 Forth to the battle! Hold your banners high;
Raise the Red Dragon to the sky!
Blow loud the bugle, never sound retreat,
Ever go onward marching feet.
Blessings be on our courageous men,
Valiant and fearless, now as then.
Make a joyful noise along the way,
Victory's before us on this great day.

From your Slumber Arise!

Codiad yr Haul

English words by Walter Maynard

2 Soaring high in the air,
   O hear the joyous birds declare,
   The light of the dawning of day is begun,
   Foreshadowing the rising of the sun,
   The beautiful rising of the sun!
   O'er high mountains gleaming,

Tingeing ev'ry hilltop with gold,
Through deep valleys streaming,
Bringing joy to young and old;
You cannot know the great delight
In watching the dreary shadows of night
Dispelled by the rays of morning light!

God Bless the Prince of Wales

Ei Bendith ar ei Ben

English words by George Linley, adapted by Margery Hargest Jones
Music by Brinley Richards

1. A-mong our an-cient moun-tains, And from our love-ly vales, Oh let us sing to-ge-ther, 'God bless the Prince of Wales!' With heart and voice re-mem-ber Those songs of long a-go, In

2 If enemies or danger
  Should threaten our fair isle,
  May God's great arm protect us,
  May Heav'n still on us smile!
  Above the throne of England
  May fortune's star still shine,
  And round our beauteous Kingdom
  The olive branches twine.
  Among our ancient mountains,
  And from our lovely vales,
  Oh let us sing together,
  'God bless the Prince of Wales!'

The Hall of My Chieftain

Ystafell Cynddylan

English words by Mrs Hemans

This poem is attributed to Heledd, daughter of Cyndrwyn, whose brothers were all killed during the troubled years following the building of King Offa's Dyke, between 757 and 796. Her lament is for her favourite brother, Cynddylan.

1. The hall of my chief - tain is emp - ty to - night; I weep, for the room has been robbed of its light: The glow from the lamp in the ceil - ing is o'er, The blaze from the hearth shall say wel - come no more.

36

2 The hall of my chieftain is silent and still,
  The sound of its sweet harp has died on the hill;
  Be quiet forever, you desolate scene,
  Nor ever an echo recall what has been.

3 The hall of my chieftain is lonely and bare,
  No banquet, no guest, not a footstep is there!
  Oh! where are the warriors who circled its board?
  The grass will soon wave where the mead-cup was poured.

4 The hall of my chieftain is gloomy tonight,
  Since he is departed whose smile made it bright;
  I mourn, but my sadness of heart shall be brief,
  As I make my way to the grave of my chief.

If She Were Mine

Pe Cawn i Hon

English words by Walter Maynard

she were mine, and__ loved me well, Life would no-thing be __ but plea-sure; I__

would not care for__ sacks of gold, Nor__ o-ther earth - ly trea-sure. Her__

win-ning ways, her laugh-ing eyes, Throw such a charm a - bout her; She__

must be mine, yes___ mine a-lone, I___ can-not live with-out her.

After Verse 2

2 If she were mine, my aim would be
To make her love me dearly,
That all her heart and all her thoughts
Belonged to me sincerely;
But should I find to my dismay
I had good cause to doubt her,
Then were she mine, yet loved me not,
I'd rather be without her!

In the Vale of Llangollen

Yn Nyffryn Llangollen

English words by Mrs Grant
Air 'The Crystal Ground'

In 1778 two Irish ladies selected Llangollen as their future home and built Plas Newydd. They lived there for about fifty years, their powers of conversation and somewhat eccentric reputation drawing scores of interesting visitors. Plas Newydd is still famous as the home of the 'Ladies of Llangollen'.

1. In the Vale of Llan - go - llen a mansion is seen, Well shel - tered from wea - ther by trees e - ver green. There the dai - sy first o - pens its eye to the day, And the

haw-thorn first blooms in the mer-ry month of May, There the dai-sy__ first o-pens its eye__ to__ the__ day,__ And the haw-thorn first blooms in the mer-ry month of May.

After Verse 2

2 There, far from the haunts of ambition and pride,
  Contentment and virtue and friendship abide;
  And nature contentedly smiles on the pair
  Of ladies who decided to worship her there;
  And nature contentedly smiles on the pair
  Of ladies who decided to worship her there.

The Lady of Sker

Y Ferch O'r Scer

Welsh words anon.
English words by Maria X. Hayes
Music by Thomas Evans

The second verse is evidently the reply made by the 'Maid of Sker' to her lover's appeal in the first verse. Sker is the name of an ancient farmhouse near the Sker Rocks, Glamorganshire, at one time inhabited by the maid with whom the composer fell hopelessly in love.

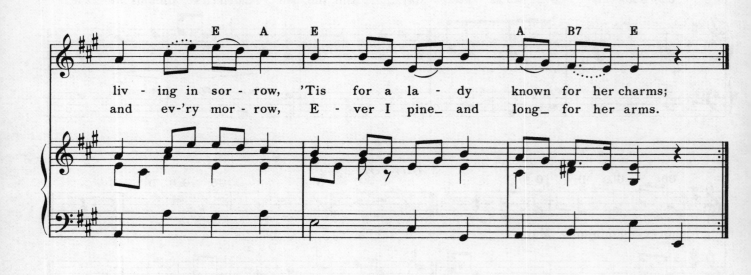

1. I am a young man living in sor - row, 'Tis for a la - dy known for her charms;
Too well I love her and ev'ry mor - row, E - ver I pine_ and long_ for her arms.

Bet - ter it is to_ show my_ pas - sion, Than to en - dure_ this_

rest - less_ pain; Come bright star, beam kind - ly_ on_ me,

Then shall my pure love be near me a-gain.

After Verse 2

D.C.

2 So does the wild young man implore me,
   I fear my hand must yet be bound;
   So many warnings are before me,
   From married lovers all around.
   I'm too young to be tied to another,
   I must make discretion my guide;
   When I am ready to take a lover
   You shall hear how I decide.

Land of My Fathers

Hen wlad fy nhadau

Welsh words by Evan James
English words by Margery Hargest Jones
Music by James James

This is the Welsh National Anthem and as such should always be sung in Welsh. However, it is also a lovely song in English, the words conveying the love of the Welsh for their native land. The melody and Welsh words, written in 1856, first appeared in John Owen's *Gems of Welsh Melody* in 1860.

1. O land of my fa-thers, O land that I__
Mae hen wlad fy nhad-au yn an-wyl i__

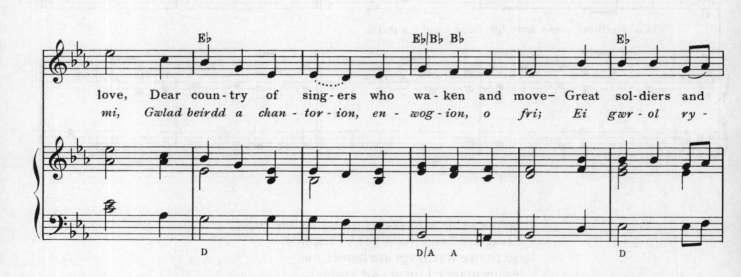

love, Dear coun-try of sing-ers who wa-ken and move- Great sol-diers and
mi, Gwlad beirdd a chan-tor-ion, en-wog-ion, o fri; Ei gwr-ol ry-

states-men to__ fight for our__ good, Our he-roes for free-dom shed blood._____
-fel-wyr, gwlad gar-wyr tra__ mâd, Dros rydd-id goll-as-ant eu gwaed._____

2 O land of great mountains, a bard's paradise
Of gentle green valleys and cliffs to the skies;
Through country so charming, through
    murmuring trees,
Flow heavenly rivers and seas.
    Wales! Wales!
    No other land can compare!
    As long as the sea your fortress shall be,
    My heart will always be there.

3 For though the oppressor may ravage your
    realm,
The language of old he cannot o'erwhelm,
Nor hinder the poet, nor music betray;
The harp strings forever shall play.
    Chorus

2 Hên Gymru fynyddig, paradwys y bardd,
Pob dyffryn, pob clogwyn, i'm golwg sydd
    hardd,
Trwy deimlad gwladgarol mor swynol yw si
Ei nentydd, afonydd i mi.
    Gwlad, Gwlad, pleidiol wyf i'm gwlad,
    Tra môr yn fur
    I'r bur hoff bau,
    O bydded i'r heniaith bar hau.

3 Os treisiodd y gelyn fy ngwlad dan ei droed,
Mae heniaith y Cymry mor fyw ag erioed;
Ni luddiwyd yr awen gan erchyll law brad,
Na thelyn berseiniol fy ngwlad.
    Chorus

Let Now the Harp

Pant Corlan yr Wyn

English words by Walter Maynard

now the_ harp and voice u - nite; Their har - mon - ies so full of skill Shall

give all_ sons of Wales de - light, Each heart with rap - ture fill. Let

first the harp the_ tune be - gin, A - lone up - on its_ trem - bling chords, And

then the voice come chim-ing in, In tune-ful mea-sure wed to words; The

two shall then to-ge-ther blend, Till words and mu-sic end.

2 Wherever harp and voice are heard
Their noblest song be ever true,
Each cheering note and thrilling word
In praise, dear land, of you.
The harp your spirit shall inspire,
Whatever hand may sweep the strings;
The voice will in your cause aspire
To stir the heart whoever sings;
And make their noblest song so true,
In praise, dear land, of you.

Loudly Proclaim

Cariwyd y Dydd

This is a song of freedom.

English words adapted by Margery Hargest Jones

1. Loud-ly pro-claim, we must be free! This is the land ___ of li-ber-ty! To win the day to-ge-ther we would fight: ___ Free-dom is our aim and ___ free-dom our right! All who may come this way

e - ver shall see___ Home of the brave, home of the free;

This is the land___ of li-ber-ty!

2 High are the hills, green are the vales,
Pure are the rivers that run in Wales;
Though long ago, our country fought in vain,
We now live in peace, and peaceful will remain.
Though we roam, this our home shall forever be –
Home of the brave, home of the free;
This is the land of liberty!

A Lovely Lady Softly Sighed

Erddigan hun Gwenlliam

English words by Walter Maynard
Air 'Gwenllian's Repose'

The 'lady' is Gwenllian, daughter of Rhys ab Gruffydd, Prince of South Wales, and the first wife of Ednyfed Fychan, chief counsellor of Llewellyn ab Iorweth, Prince of North Wales. She was eminent among the members of her handsome and clever family for her beauty and intelligence. She died in 1236.

1. A love-ly la-dy soft-ly sigh'd, 'O come, my on-ly love, to me, O come, my on-ly love, my on-ly love, to me!' Though young men sought her for their bride, And vow'd to be faith-ful and true, faith-ful and

50

true; But still the la - dy e - ver sigh'd, 'My love, I live or die for you, My love, I live for you, I live or die for you.'

2 In brightest days of summertime,
  'O come, my only love, to me,
  O come, my only love, my only love, to me!'
  And when the bells up in the steeple chime,
  Her prayer is lifted high above, high above;
  In darkest days of wintertime,
  'I know I live or die for love,
  I know I live for love, I live or die for love!'

3 She lived though pining through the years,
  'O come, my only love, to me,
  O come, my only love, my only love, to me!'
  Though she had shed so many, many tears
  For one she loved so faithfully, so faithfully.
  At rest, now from her hopes and fears
  She sleeps beneath the willow tree,
  She sleeps beneath the willow, 'neath the willow tree.

The Marsh of Rhuddlan

Morfa Rhuddlan

Welsh words and music anon.
English words by Maria X. Hayes

Tradition has always held that this song commemorates the great battle under Offa of Mercia and Caradoc. The real origin is unknown. It is the lament of a nation broken-hearted under a great disaster.

1. Dark is the_ day and so dread-ful_ the_ sto-ry, When foes did_ con-quer the_ sons of the free. At our de-struc-tion the sun hid_ his_ glo-ry, Swords of_ the_ e-ne-my were all we could see. Wild ban-dits

Believe Me, If All Those Endearing Young Charms

Words by Thomas Moore
Music traditional

2 It is not while beauty and youth are thine own,
And thy cheeks unprofan'd by a tear,
That the fervour and faith of a soul can be known,
To which time will but make thee more dear!
No, the heart that has truly lov'd never forgets,
But as truly loves on to the close;
As the sunflower turns on her god when he sets
The same look which she turn'd when he rose.

11

Megan's Fair Daughter

Merch Megan

English words by John Oxenford

*) Pronounced 'Rhuthlan'

2 Deep may the marsh be o'erwhelmed by the ocean,
Open, oh Neptune, the gates of the deep.
Fast on the harps of our bards tears are flowing,
Rise up among us, O Lord, never sleep!
Once more I'll gaze on the dark scene of slaughter,
Freedom unconquered but sleeps in her grave;
Better to die beneath Rhuddlan's ancient water,
Calm is that sleep for the sons of the brave.

2 When I go to sleep, for you I am praying,
   I'm ever, dear maid, with you at my side.
   You hear with delight the words I am saying,
   You know that my heart is bursting with pride.
   But when I'm awake, if I say I adore you,
   Your look ever tells me my love is in vain;
   I'll see you no more, nor worry, nor haunt you;
   I know in my dreams, you'll love me again.

Men of Harlech

Rhyfelgyrch Gwyr Harlech

English words by Margery Hargest Jones

This has invariably been seen as a 'march to battle' song, whereas in fact it refers to the siege of Harlech Castle. King Edward IV of England ordered the Earl of Pembroke to lead a powerful army to demand the surrender of the castle. Famine finally defeated the brave Welshmen, who made an 'honourable capitulation'.

1. Men of Har - lech, this your sto - ry, How you brave - ly live for glo - ry,
You de - fend your cas - tle's tow - er, To pro - tect our coun - try's flow - er,

And you fight for free - dom sure - ly Bat - tle of the brave!
As they brave the ar - rows' show - er, Har - lech for to

save. All the land a - wak - ing, Hill and val - ley shak - ing;

56

2 Though the foe is e'er attacking,
And the castle walls are cracking,
There is never courage lacking,
Fighting to the death!
Though your men are sick and dying,
And your loved ones sad and crying,
Freedom in the flag is flying,
Till your final breath!
All the mountains ringing,
Every valley singing;
As you fight with all your might
To faith and hope you're clinging;
With the foe towards you leaping,
You your valiant stance are keeping;
All the nation with you weeping,
Freedom will not die!

The Miller's Daughter

Merch y Melinydd

English words by Walter Maynard

am the mill-er's daugh - ter, And when the mill goes round, I lis - ten to its

mur - mur, As to a warn - ing sound; Ad - vice it seems to give me, As

would a dear old friend, And tells me of the dan - gers With which I must con -

-tend.

2. It

2 It tells me to be thrifty,
   And not to waste a day,
   And how the precious moments
   Of life soon pass away.
   I may not always hear it,
   But where my home may be,
   The mill's familiar murmur
   Will be a guide to me.

The Missing Boat

Yn Nyffryn Clwyd

English words by Walter Maynard

60

-turn since then.

2 The skipper's wife goes down
   Ev'ry day from the town,
   To watch for tidings on the shore;
   She strains her aching eyes,
   And through her tears she spies
   The phantom of a boat that will come back no more.

3 The child there on her arm,
   Unaware of alarm,
   Asks, 'When will father come again?'
   The mother won't reply,
   But with a heavy sigh,
   She longs for his return but knows she hopes in vain.

The Morning Glory

Y march a'r gwddw brith

English words adapted by Margery Hargest Jones

62

2 And thoughts were on them creeping,
  Of dear ones left at home,
  Who would for them be weeping,
  Afraid to be alone.
  But each man was his brother,
  And conscience led them to the fray,
  For victory to be won that day,
  They may not see another;
  For victory to be won that day,
  They may not see another.

My Heart
Fy Nghalon

English words by John Thomas

1. My heart, I have lived in this world, and I know That love just like hat-red is tint-ed with woe; Oh pa-rents of child-ren, of lo-ver and friend, How soon is af-fec-tion in sad-ness to end?

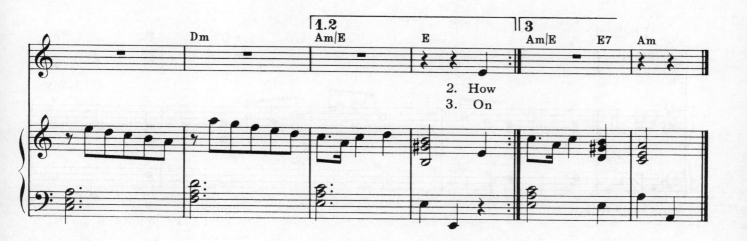

2 How pleasant to meet with our loved ones it is,
And what heart than my heart knows better of this?
But now when the loved ones can meet me no more,
My heart in its anguish will feel so sore.

3 On mountain, in valley, by fountain and grove,
How lovely the greetings of friendship did prove!
Now lonely I wander with only my heart
To tell me in pity we meet but to part.

My Lady Is More Fair

Ffani Blodau'r ffair

Welsh words traditional
English words adapted by Margery Hargest Jones

praise _____ Of her, though_ words can ne - ver say_ What

charms with-in her lay.

After Verse 2

2 The River Neath shall course
  Back from the ocean to its source,
  If my poor foolish will
  Should change through good or ill;
  Though time itself grows old,
  Yet my poor heart will not grow cold
  Towards the girl for whom I care,
  My lady is so fair!

New Year's Eve

Nos Galan

English words by Margery Hargest Jones

This is an old secular carol celebrating the coming of the new year.

1 Now the old year soon is end-ing,
New Year greet-ings we are send-ing, *Fal, la, la, la, la, la, la, la, la.*

To our friends and our re-la-tions, *Fal, la, la, la, la, la, la, la,*

Wish-ing peace to all the na-tions, *Fal, la, la, la, la, la, la, la, la.*

2 May the new year bring us gladness,
    Fal, la, la, la, la, la, la, la, la.
May it wipe away all sadness,
    Fal, la, la, la, la, la, la, la, la.
Fill the cup and hang the holly,
    Fal, la, la, la, la, la, la, la,
'Tis the season to be jolly,
    Fal, la, la, la, la, la, la, la, la.

O Mountain White

Eryri Wen

English words by Margery Hargest Jones

Snowdon has always been a powerful symbol in Wales: as early as 1230 Llewelyn the Great proclaimed himself Lord of Eryri (Snowdonia).

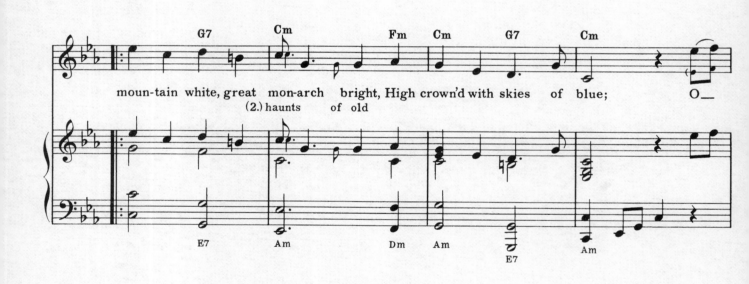

70

tales of old your sons have told, Of the fear-ful power you bear, With-

-in your cloud-y co-ver-let, We see you stand-ing there!

2. Tho'

2 Tho' from their stormy haunts of old
   Your eagles long have flown;
   Yet still our hearts shall fly as high
   Above your mountain throne.
   And then our song, all ages long,
   Will linger in the air,
   And round your snowy peaks we'll see
   White Snowdon standing there!

The Old Year Is Passing

Mae'r Flwyddyn yn Marw

English words by Margery Hargest Jones

1. The old year is pass-ing its hours a-way, And clouds in the sky now will co-ver the day. The night-winds are sigh-ing, the last min-ute near, The bells are all si-lent, fare-well to the

2 But here is the new year to make our hearts gay,
As everyone welcomes another new day.
The young and the old folk are dancing with joy,
And the bells will be ringing for each girl and boy.

3 To welcome the new year our carol we sing,
To autumn and winter, to summer and spring.
May peace and contentment be with us always,
For year after year to the end of our days.

On This Day

Difyrwch y Brenin

English words by John Oxenford
Air 'The King's Delight'

1. On this day our King was born, Let harp be sound-ed— till the morn;
Fill the cup up to— the brim, For ev-'ry heart de-lights in him.

Bards with— voi-ces— clear and— strong, Pour free-ly forth a—

joy - ous song; Cheer-ing— day and glad-d'ning night, And call your song 'The

2 For the King well pleased will be,
  While listening to the melody
  Being sung by one and all,
  In lowly cottage, lofty hall.
  May he live a thousand years,
  And may this song ever please his ears;
  May his smile be always bright
  When he has heard 'The King's Delight'.

Once a Farmer and His Wife

Y saith Gyscadur

English words by Walter Maynard

This song is said to have been a favourite of Henry V (1387-1422) when he was the Prince of Wales, and used to be sung by the Prince and his companions at the Boar's Head Tavern, Cheapside.

1. Once a farm-er and his wife_ Had cause for dis-pu-ta - tion;

They were used_ to noi-sy strife, And word-y al-ter-ca-tion;

'Good-man,' said she, 'You are too free, And too o-pen-hand-ed.'

'Good-wife,' said he, 'You let me be, I will not be com-mand-ed!'

2 Then when harvest time came round,
   And boys with girls were racing,
   Oft the farmer's wife had found
   He would the girls be chasing.
   'Good-man,' cried she, 'you are too free,
   And too open-hearted.'
   'Good-wife,' said he, 'you let me be,
   Or we will soon be parted.'

3 Long, long years did pass away,
   And still they kept on railing,
   Till at last, one winter's day,
   She said, when she was ailing,
   'I am too old always to scold,
   I think your ways are mended.'
   Said he, 'You're right, you are quite right,'
   And so the matter ended.

One Bright Summer Morning

Cadair Idris

English words by Margery Hargest Jones
Air 'Jenny Jones' by John Parry

1. One bright sum-mer morn-ing, when day-light was dawn-ing, The sun-rise was sprink-ling the mount-ains with gold; While down in the val-ley, my beau-ti-ful Jen-ny Was wait-ing for me to re-turn to the fold. When she was a young girl, up

there would she wan-der, And walk those fair hills which we see from our home; Though now she is old-er, she'll climb them no long-er, But stay in our cot-tage, no more will she roam.

After Verse 2

2 So down from the castle which crosses the river,
I feel my heart aching and longing for her;
My feet have to hurry to meet with my Jenny,
And tell her I love her and dry every tear.
The bells in the steeple ring out o'er the meadow,
Rejoicing with us on our white wedding day;
I'll marry my Jenny and keep her forever,
So safely together in love will we stay.

Over the Stone

Tros y Garreg

English words by John Oxenford
Music c. 1485

This beautiful song possibly dates from 1485, when Rhys Bodychen led the men of Anglesey to and from the Battle of Bosworth.

80

friend have been; Some for-get__ me, some have fled, Some are false and some__ are dead; Chang-ing ne - ver, con - stant e - ver Here for-e - ver, brave old stone.

2 Standing there, O silent stone,
What a world you must have known!
Brave men dying, women crying,
Children lying – left to moan.
Here beneath the grass it's said,
Many a soldier's bones are laid;
Fighting for their land they fell,
None but you the rest can tell;
Secrets keeping, ever sleeping,
Guardian of the past alone.

The Rising of the Lark

Codiad yr Hedydd

English words by Maria X. Hayes

1 Hark! Hark! his morn-ing praise, In gen-tle song the lark will raise To
Are they the pearls of song Dropped by a count-less an-gel throng, When

pa-ra-dise a-bove;
bring-ing peace and love? Calm the breeze a-cross the moor, Nor

does the pur-ple hea-ther blow; And the brook will stop to hear, While hid-ing in the

rush-es there, The heav'n-ly, plea-sant, ten-der sound That's charm-ing to the

ear.

2 Rise, rise, fly up in space
On soft grey wing from place to place
And ever high above.
Sing, sing your sweetest song,
Fly nearer to that happy throng
Who bring us peace and love.
Sing and let the whole world hear
Your melody so loud and clear;
Waking longing in mankind
To chase your voice to heaven above;
Nearer to day and nearer God
Eternal joy to find.

Sad was the Day

Difyrwch gwyr Dyfi

English words by George Linley

1. Sad was the day when her smile I first met, Nor will my heart__ that mo-ment for-get; Cap - tive soon like some__ poor bird, With ev - 'ry__ soft__ and win - ning word; I__ thought her an an - gel with - out__ dis-guise, Nor

dreamed that de - ceit_ could dwell in those eyes.

2 Now she is mine – by her beauty betrayed,
I see at last the mistake I have made;
Cold, inconstant too I find,
A face of smiles, a spirit unkind;
Young lover, you take this advice then from me,
Be deaf while you hear, be blind while you see.

So Early in the Morning

Y Bore Glas

English words by Maria X. Hayes

day.

2. I

2 I loved to hear his love-song,
   And waited there for so long;
   I would with my affection
   His gift to me repay;
   Truly his enchanting trilling
   My joyful heart was thrilling
   With his love-song, tenderly at break of day.

Springtime Is Returning
Breuddwyd y Frenhines

English words by Walter Maynard, adapted by Margery Hargest Jones

1. Spring-time is re-turn - ing, the__ win-ter cold and
Birds sing in the branch - es where bud - ding leaves are

grey With snow and nip-ping frost will soon have passed a - way;
seen, And ev - 'ry dus - ky hedge is tint - ed o'er with green.

Now no more a - far is heard the hunt-er's wind-ing horn,__ And with care the

far - mer guards his fields at ear - ly morn;— Spring-time is re - turn - ing the

win - ter cold and grey With snow and nip-ping frost will soon have passed a - way.

After Verse 2

2 Softly blows the south wind along the hills and vales,
While merrily the streams flow through the sunny dales;
Flocks now leave the mountains to browse among the fields
And feed on luscious meadows happy springtime yields.
Soon the new born lambs will gambol in the morning dew
And the blossom in the hedgerows will enhance the view;
Springtime is returning, the winter cold and grey
With snow and nipping frost will soon have passed away.

The Stars Above Are Bright

Mentra Gwen

English words by Walter Maynard

1. The stars a-bove are bright, La-dy mine, La-dy mine; The moon is full to-night,__ La-dy__ mine. Oh! will you e-ver hear me, Or come to love me dear-ly? I need you e-ver near me, Long-ing

for you, La - dy mine.

2. The
3. Let

8....:

2 The wind is passing by,
Lady mine, Lady mine,
And brings you many a sigh,
Lady mine;
The flowers now are sleeping,
While all the world is weeping,
But I my watch am keeping,
Longing for you, Lady mine.

3 Let not my longing seem,
Lady mine, Lady mine,
A hopeless, passing dream,
Lady mine;
Look now my love, and hear me,
I want you ever near me
And love you oh most dearly,
Longing for you, Lady mine.

There Lived a Bachelor

Ap Siencyn

Welsh words by T. Tudno Jones
English words by Margery Hargest Jones
Music by John Parry

1. There lived a ba-che-lor long a-go,— As bright as a bird on his fa-ther's land; De-spite the ar-rows of Cu-pid's bow,— He ne-ver did ask for a la-dy's hand. His hor-ses, cat-tle, fields and purse, Were want-ed by ma-ny, as I've been told, But

still he thought it might be worse, If mar-ried to one who'd be bought with gold; So the

ba - che-lor was with-out much strife, He shared his mo-ney with all the poor, And

if he left___ no child nor wife, His name___ would live while the harp strings soar!

2 He loved the country life he led,
   With hunting and fishing and peaceful joys,
   His crops and animals to be fed,
   No sons or daughters to make a noise.
   He journeyed through his life alone,
   Until it came to his last long sleep,
   And was content that he had known
   No wife nor child to leave to weep;
   So the bachelor was without much strife,
   He shared his money with all the poor,
   And if he left no child nor wife,
   His name would live while the harp strings soar.

This Garden Now
I blas Gogerddan

English words by Walter Maynard

'Gogerddan' is an ancient mansion near Aberystwyth.

1. This gar - den, now so de - so - late, Was tend - ed once with care; And
   bloom-ing flow'rs with - in its gate, With per - fume filled the
   air. Then of - ten there fond pro - mi - ses Were made of youth - ful love, By lov - ers now be - neath the shade Of yon - der cy - press

grove,____ By lov - ers now be - neath the shade Of yon - der__ cy - press grove.

2. When

2 When ruined by relentless fate,
  The joy by lovers known,
  Then as this garden desolate,
  Is life on earth alone.
  But hope will then much stronger grow
  And all its power prove
  To lovers now on earth below
  Of greater joy above;
  To lovers now on earth below
  Of greater joy above.

Watching the Wheat

Bugeilio'r Gwenith Gwyn

English words by Margery Hargest Jones

The words to this most popular and famous of Welsh airs tell the hapless love story of Will Hopkin, a Bard in the 1770s. He wrote many songs in honour of Ann Thomas (the Maid of Cefu Ydfa).

1. In my young and fool-ish days I fell in love for - e - ver, And she was young and fool-ish too— We fell in love _____ to- -ge-ther. As we strolled the coun-try lanes And saw the wheat there

blow-ing; We lit-tle thought what life would bring, Or

where our love____ was go-ing.

2 Pure and lovely were the days
When we had faith together,
As we walked hand in hand among
The hills of purple heather.
For the sake of my sweet love,
So merciful and tender,
I'll always keep her cheerful smile
Locked in my heart forever.

Weep Not for Me

Serch Hudol

English words by John Oxenford

more than life or love. Now I_ see you smile, Your sad-ness you would so be-guile, You

weep, yet cheer me on, the while, Fare - well, dear love, fare - well: I

know the ach - ing in your heart– It's sad for_ you that I de - part– Will

match the ach - ing in my heart, Fare - well, dear love, fare - well!

2 Anger awake, all bonds to break,
Never shall our hearts forsake
The rage that speaks aloud,
While one invader can be found
Whose foot pollutes our holy ground,
That smiled on us when fortune frowned,
So fearless and so proud.

3 Opening every eye, the fury that will never die,
Until we make the foe to fly,
And bring us back to love,
The love for country and for all
That faithful hearts their own would call,
A love that n'er again will fall,
That nothing is above.

Well I Know

Dwfn yw'r môr

English words by Margery Hargest Jones

in the sun, Vow - ing love with all__ our might; But the swal - lows

long have flown, Bear - ing on__ their wings my bliss; Oth - er hearts your

love now own, Oth - er lips__ may claim your kiss.

After Verse 2

2 Sweetly shine your loving eyes,
   But they shine no more for me;
   Melting tears in mine arise,
   Bitter as the briny sea.
   'I will be your faithful one,
   Long as swallows take their flight;'
   So we stood here in the sun,
   Vowing love with all our might.
   Here once more the swallows fly,
   Skimming through the sunlit skies;
   All I hear is winter's sigh,
   Never more to see your eyes.

When I Was Roaming

Pan O'wn i'n Rhodio

Welsh words traditional
English words by Maria X. Hayes

1. When I was roam-ing in the gloam-ing Of a love-ly sum-mer day, Two were walk-ing, two were talk-ing, And I heard the la - dy say: 'All your woo-ing, all pur-su-ing, Will ne - ver win_ this

heart of mine; The wa - ters e - ver find___ their le - vel,

Ne - ver will___ your heart___ find mine.'

After Verse 2

2 The young man sighing, then replying:
'I think all the world of you;
Fame I heed not, wealth I need not,
I have all if you'd be true;
Do not hurt me, or desert me,
Do not let me ask in vain;
Oh tell your heart to show me pity,
Never condemn me to live in pain.'

When Morning Is Breaking

Pan gyfyd yr Heulwen

English words by Walter Maynard

tell_ the_ great glad - ness of_ all the_ day_ long.

2. When

2 When evening is closing over mountain and vale,
   The darkness descends on our home in the dale.
   The wild flowers drooping, the fast fading light,
   Give warning of sadness, the approaching of night.

Why Do I Just Gaze?

Wrth edrych yn ol

English words by Mrs Hemans
Air 'Lady Owen's Delight'

This song may refer to Prince Madoc, born in North Wales between 1134 and 1142. He was an explorer and possibly landed in America around 1170. He supposedly found a land 'affording health, aire, gold, good water and plenty of nature's blessings'.

2 Why do I hear clear those sweet songs of my land,
Where the sound of the harp on each wild wind is borne?
O hush you sweet sound, be still with your hand
You harper whose melody greets every morn!
Oh no! let your echoes still float on the breeze,
And my heart shall be strong for the crossing of seas.

3 The land of my fathers would never give birth
To men who lack valour when ventures are near!
We will carry away o'er ocean and earth
A name and a spirit without any fear;
I'll be guided by stars, by winds set my course,
But my heart, my dear country, will always be yours.

Reproduced and printed by
Halstan & Co. Ltd., Amersham, Bucks., England

Index to the titles in Welsh